HELLO BABY!

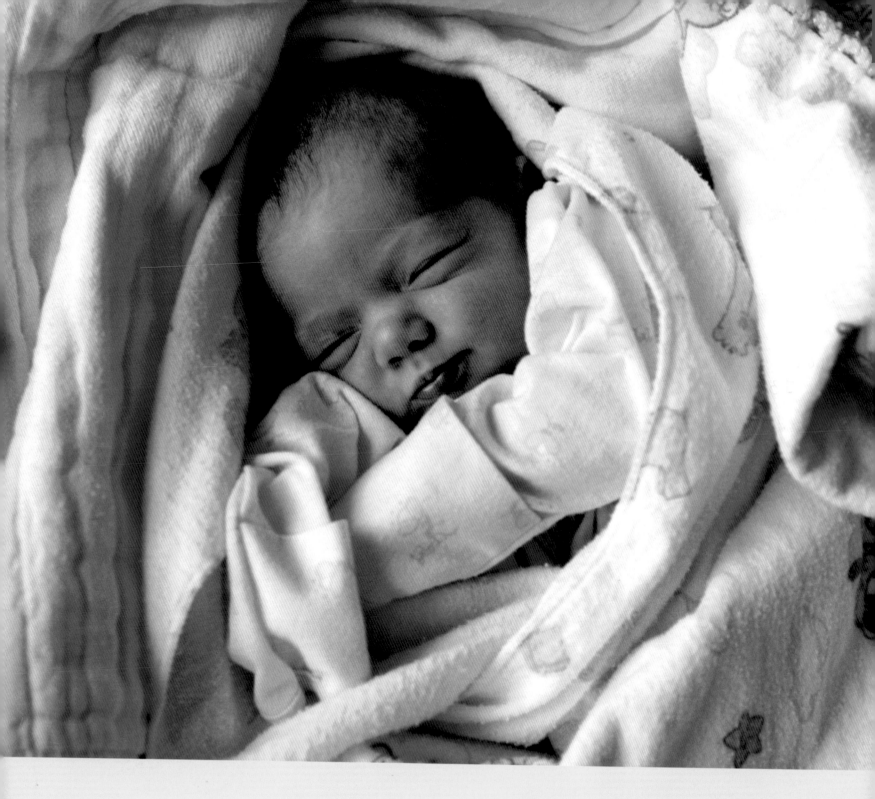

Look! A brand new baby in a blanket: a European baby kept all cosy and warm.

Snoozing baby. Shhh, baby's asleep. This baby from Burma is fast asleep.

Swinging from the ceiling, wrapped in some cloth; this Indonesian baby is being rocked to sleep.

Rock-a-bye baby in his hammock; this Mongolian baby is quiet and calm.

A hungry baby from Panama, drinking his mother's milk.
Holding on tight, he doesn't want to let go.

See the Thai baby, slurping from a bottle; drinking down milk to grow big and strong.

Feed the little girl with a spoon. This **Caribbean** girl is having soft, mushy food.

A Vietnamese child being fed some rice; this child has teeth
and finds rice is nice!

Bath time, baby! Now for some open-air washing in an Indonesian river.

Bath time is fun here in Japan; swimming and clinging or just hanging on.

A baby in a bucket? Well, why not! This Nepalese baby thinks it's perfect if the water's not too hot.

It's fun in the bath when you are surrounded by toys.
That's what this baby in the United Kingdom likes.

Time for a check up, baby. The nurse checks a baby in Senegal - thank you baby, everything looks fine.

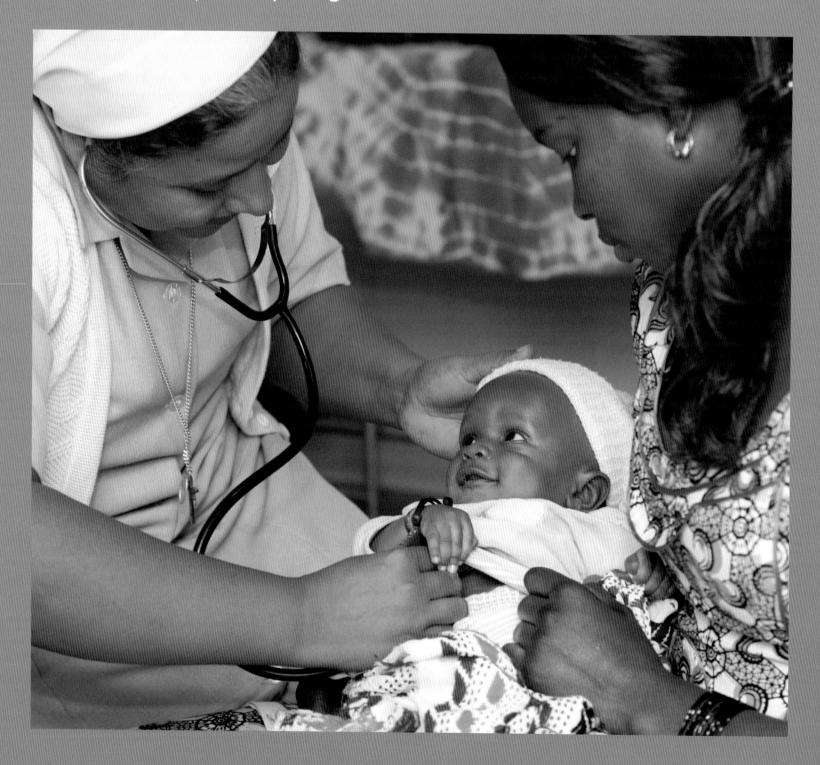

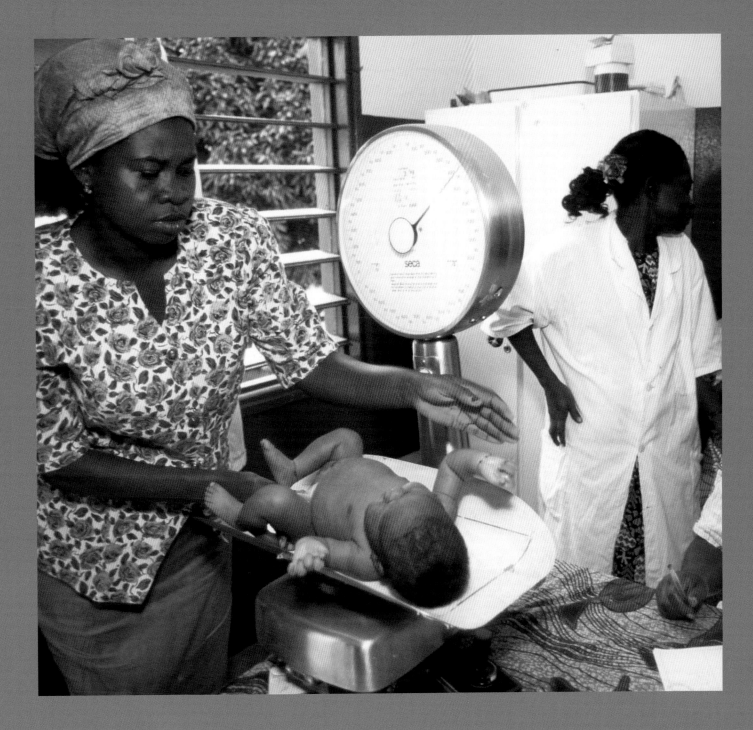

How much do you weigh? Babies grow up fast; here in Gabon a baby is being weighed. Look how heavy you are!

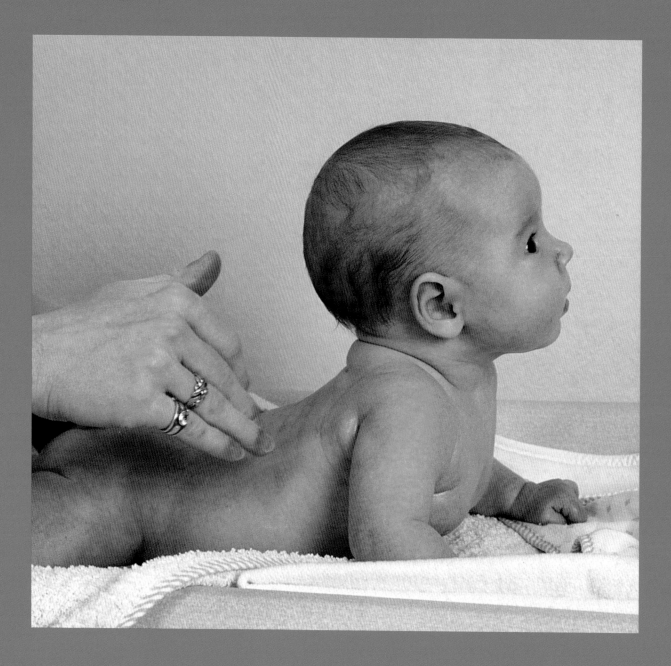

Oooh, babies love a massage! A soft, gentle rub makes this European baby smile.

In Nepal too, a massage goes down a treat. This baby is so relaxed ... he's even gone to sleep!

Baby on the move; getting a ride from his mother.
This Peruvian baby is being carried in a sling.

Now here are two enjoying the view. In Burma a mother balances both her children in baskets.

Playtime, baby! In Guinea-Bissau a baby scoops up soil with a spoon – it's fun to play with, but not to eat.

Peek-a-boo baby! Who's that looking back? A baby in America

Off to work! In Madagascar a baby sits in a sling while his mother works – it's tiring stuff.

School time, baby – but surely you're too young! Not in Mali
when the teacher is your mum!

Come and meet the family; a Peruvian baby with
her mum, dad, brother and sister.

Everyone wants to see the baby. In Niger, the whole family comes to visit this new little one.

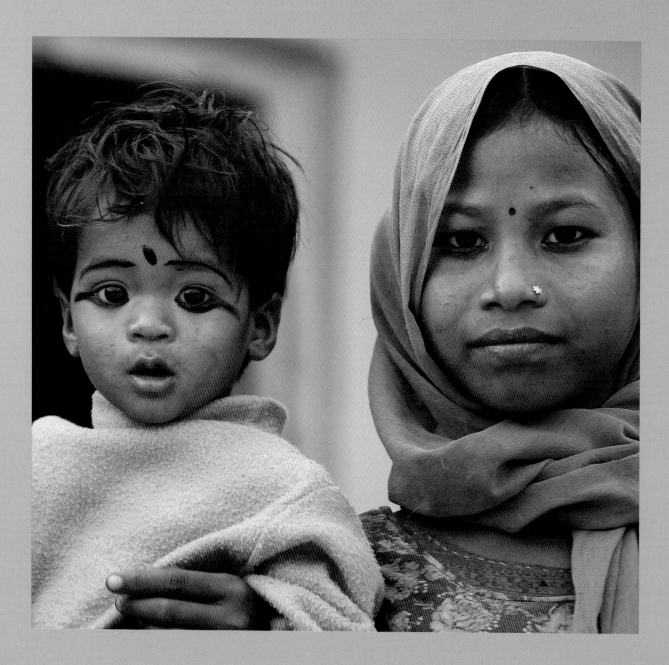

Looking good, baby! An Indian boy wears traditional face paint.

Face-painted children from Burma. The paint they use is made from trees.

All aboard baby! Chinese babies travelling home in style.

Bye-bye babies ...